I0149200

SEASONS of WAR by Dr. Marlene Miles

Freshwater Press, USA

Webpage: marlenemilestheauthor.com

https://www.instagram.com/marlenemilestheauthor/

ISBN: 978-1-960150-46-2

Paperback Version

Table of Contents

SEASONS of WAR

Freshwater

Why Am I Under Attack?

You're saved so you may be wondering why life is coming at you like it is. *Why am I under attack?* you might ask.

The Lord is a man of war. The LORD is a man of war; the LORD is his name, (Exodus 15:3). God is raising up sons and sons are brought up to be like their fathers.

Jesus was the first born of many brethren and God is still raising up sons. The whole Earth is groaning and waiting for the *sons* of God to appear. Are you one of them? Are you *becoming* a **son** of God?

Because you're saved you now have the *authority* to become a son of God is why you are so interesting to the devil. If the enemy has his eye on you, you either *are* a son of God, or you are *becoming* a son of God. It's why the devil has made you a target. Whatever God is interested in building up, the devil is interested in tearing down. And vice versa. This has been true since the beginning of time.

As a newborn, Jesus had Herod's attention. Jesus, the firstborn Son of God, was a sure threat to the devil. By demonic influence Herod was put on the path to track down the infant. The devil knew Jesus' destiny--, it was in that magnificent star that Herod's magicians no doubt had spied out.

We humans all have stars, we each are also destined to become a son of God. That's why you fall under attack. War has been declared on you because the devil never stops. Just as the devil in Herod hated Jesus, the devil may find another human to influence against *you*. That's *how* you're under attack.

If attacked by the devil you will remain under attack until he captures you, destroys your destiny, or you. Or, **until you stop him**.

You have a destiny in the Lord, you have a purpose on Earth which you will fulfill as a son. God is raising up sons under stiff opposition.

No curse can alight without a cause, so many don't worry about what the devil is doing because they believe they are sin-free. Denying that there is a cause won't change the fact that you may be attractive to curses. Others are sincerely unaware of anything that would cause the devil to declare war on them. Whether the cause is generational or foundational, or if it's your own sin, a cause is still a cause.

You still have a destiny in God, so break the curse and protect your life and destiny, God is quick to forgive if you repent.

God cherishes His sons; you should be one of them.

Not A Little Boy

In the Book of Daniel, the Prince of Persia – a *whole* principality withstood the answer to Daniel's prayers. Why? Daniel was just a little Hebrew boy.

In the natural Daniel looked like a boy, but Daniel was <u>not</u> a little boy to God. Neither are you a little, helpless nobody to God. You are somebody to Him, or you are *becoming* a son because God is raising up sons. For this reason there are things that you can and should do yourself that God will not do for you. Aren't you the same way with your own children?

> And the servant abideth not in the house for ever: *but* the Son abideth forever. (John 8:35)

God has expectations of us because He knows our end from the beginning. He has plans for us, plans to prosper us and give us a future. We are saved, and under the Better

Covenant, we are no longer under the Law. We are under Grace, but we don't use Grace as an opportunity to sin. God gives us Grace while He is raising us up as sons.

Servants are under the Law, but sons are under Grace. We don't use Grace as an opportunity to do nothing, as if we are trust fund babies. We may come into the Kingdom young and naïve, but God does not expect us to stay that way--, trusting Him, yes--, but not naïve, ignorant, or stupid.

By our Covenant with Jesus Christ, we are promoted from servants to sons. A son abides in the House forever, and he abides by the rules of the House.

Going Through

If God loves me like a son, then why am I going *through*? Why am I going through so much? For many reasons, but the day has sufficient problems unto itself.

Are you praying? Consider that if you are not praying your angels *through*, then **you** will be going *through*. What is happening in the heavenlies is mirrored in the Earth.

Going through is a term the old folks used to describe going through heck and high water, going through trials, temptations, tribulations. It describes **Seasons of War** or at least a season of attack, hindrance, or setback. It describes suffering and or affliction.

As you go *through* God is teaching your hands to war. If you are not going through, you are stuck. If you are stuck, you are in captivity. So, let God teach you; put on the whole armor and do battle in the *seasons of war* of your life.

God is raising up *sons*. How would you want to raise your son? God wants His sons to be wise, discerning, know how to fight, battle, war, pray, intercede, praise, and worship, among other things.

What parent would want to say, *Oh that's my son, but he doesn't know anything?* God would not want to say, *That's my son, but he doesn't know how to do anything,* any more than you would want to say that about your child.

Or, *That's my son but I haven't been able to teach him anything.* Trust this: JESUS IS A MASTER TEACHER. If you decide to be rebellious or lazy and <u>not learn</u> what you need to *become* a *son*, that's on you. When we are saved, we are given *authority* to become sons. It is a process that takes work. Ignorant, untrained, and inexperienced equals a toddler in the Spirit. Studying to show yourself approved is part of the process; the Holy Spirit will help when you apply yourself.

The Lord protects babies, but we can't stay babies and spiritual toddlers forever.

God did not let the devil get to Jesus as an infant, a child, or a teen (that we know of). The devil rolled up on Jesus, but it wasn't until Jesus was baptized in the Jordan by Baptist John at age 30. In God's Grace and Mercy, He will keep things from us when we are young, but as time goes by, tests required for spiritual promotion may come.

Work, saints of God. Doing nothing spiritual but just living your flesh life, saying, *God has got all the spiritual stuff, I don't have to do anything else now that I'm saved.* Even your 26-year-old has to get their own health insurance and can't stay on the parents' policy forever. What *spiritual* policy are you on and how long can you stay on it before you have to do warfare **for yourself**?

Seasons of War will come. It doesn't matter how nice, kind, sweet, respectful or Godly you are, the devil will find a *Herod* to hate on you. You may not be the *cause* of the war or the warfare, but then again you may. Is it a bloodline vendetta? Whatever the reason, you must learn what to do and *do it* in *Seasons of War* because you are being raised up as a son of God, with all the rights, authority, and responsibilities.

Maybe one day you'll be one of God's great generals--,

Oh, you think you're just called to play the piano in the Kingdom. A musical instrument <u>is</u> an instrument of war. You're a flag twirler? That's also an instrument of war.

Praise and worship--, you think you're just here to sing? You are an instrument of **war-ship.** Your mouth, your voice, uttering the Word of God – an instrument of war!

Herod didn't wait until Jesus grew up; he came for Jesus as an infant. You are definitely not an infant now, but how long do you expect others to shield you or fight *for* you?

That's why you're going *through* because you're one of God's and the devil hates it. The devil wanted to take Jesus out, but God wasn't having any of that. In the natural, think of it--, a *whole* king is trying to kill a newborn baby. The realms of darkness are heartless, so you need to learn to defend yourself properly as soon as possible.

A well-seasoned, well-ordered enemy, with personnel and who is full of evil could be after you. You'd better learn how to deal in seasons of war, especially if you just got saved last week. Or maybe you got saved 12 years ago, but all this praying and warfare stuff is not for you. Yeah, you're still a newborn in the Spirit. We've learned from Herod's killing all the male children under two years old when coming after Jesus that he doesn't mind collateral damage.

Maybe the warfare you're experiencing isn't even aimed at you, you're just too close to the battlefield. Either way, Herod doesn't care.

What 'cha gonna do?

Prophetically, the devil sees who you are to God, and he isn't willing to wait until you become spiritually full grown. The devil will even go after a newborn. Even if you are newly born into the Kingdom of God, you are still a target based on who you *will be* to God, who you **will be** in God that the enemy is after. God could be raising you up to be a weapon against the devil…

Some Weapons

Any weakness or bad habit you may have will be weaponized by the devil. Your sins, your mouth, your thought life… all can be weaponized. Saying, *No weapon formed against me will prosper* is Scriptural but make sure YOU are not helping to **form** the weapon that will be used against you. Making evil vows, evil oaths and sinning in general forms weapons against you.

Let's say a person breaks the first Commandment, if that's the same as giving the devil a gun, that you know he's going to aim at you. Why do it?

Stop that!

Then, if you break the next Commandment, that hands the devil a clip of so many bullets. And so on. Stop helping the devil. If the devil has nothing in you and surely no weapons trained on you, then there will be no seasons of war.

If you're a man who likes the ladies--, tell the truth: You like your flesh, and you like how the ladies make your flesh *feel*. You love yourself. This is idolatry. When you make sex into an idol that is sexual idolatry. That's now two idols, *yourself and sex.*

The devil now has two guns actually--, *or worse.*

What does the sex addict have? Another *date?*

The devil now has a custom weapon against you that you helped him form. The Bible is given for instruction. Three renown men of God, David, Samson, and Solomon's had the same weakness: lust. The devil weaponizes human weaknesses. What is your weakness? Don't tell me; tell God. Confess it to God. Repent. Ask God to strengthen you and to get the weakness out of you! It's a *spirit.*

Confession, repentance and resisting the devil is the only way to wrestle that weapon out of his hand. You're not alone, though. King David and King Solomon were God's men, but they were tempted by lust. They both failed. Samson's downfall was because of lust toward Delilah.

These are places where the enemy seeks to compromise, defile and trap men and women, even those *becoming* sons of God. Here comes the attack from the devil…here comes the warfare, the attacks on your marriage, education, career, wealth, children--, even your pets. As you are going *through,* don't ever think you're the only one or that you're alone. There is help! God is our ever-present help in seasons of trouble.

The man who wants everything he sees and allows himself to have it, such as food, drinks, drugs, sex – any form of immediate gratification is most at risk to fall under devil temptation of almost any kind. Sexual lust is no exception since *lust* in general is the driver of these strong desires. Over-indulged *kings,* privileged celebrities like Samson, for example are such who enjoy immediate gratification.

Part of the enemy's strategy is to make you feel as if you're the only one, and this has never happened before. Adam and Eve, the first sinners, were the only ones at that time, and they hid. But since then we've learned don't sin, but if you do, you're not alone; don't hide. Don't hide. Instead confess, repent, and join with like-minded people who have experienced this before to learn how to fight and overcome demonic oppression. There is strength in numbers.

If you are isolated in a corner the mental attack will most likely start, You know you can't tell anyone about this. They always knew you'd be a loser. Dude, you will be so embarrassed. Those are common devil taunts.

Then you may start doing worse to yourself as you talk to yourself, or to God. *God, how can this be happening? Where is God?*

Run **to** God. Tell the truth, shame the devil. You're not the only one and you're not alone. God won't turn His back on you. After confession and repentance, ask God for *more* protection, m*ore* strength. Ask God for deliverance from your temptations. Keep your prayer life up.

God will answer in your favor, but you still may have to go *through* the **season of warfare** because of the iniquity of the sin itself.

Reasons to War

A time to love, and a time to hate; a time of war, and a time of peace. Ecclesiastes 3:8

If you decide to get into a spiritual war, what are your reasons for it? What are you going to war *for*? Is it to defend yourself, your family and things that you have stewardship over? Is it because the enemy has declared war on you, so you must fight to defend yourself?

Are you fighting for peace and safety in the land, in your home? Trying to save your marriage? Career? Family, children?

This could be a defensive war or one of offence, where you've decided you're not going to wait for the devil to do more stuff to you. It could be because you've decided to annihilate the enemy because you hate him, or he hates you, and you finally realize both of those things. Is this an enemy of GOD that you know you **must** war against because of your covenant with God? Is this your own personal enemy who stole your spouse, stole your property? Is this enemy after your kids?

Is this a Ziklag situation for you; are you desirous of war to recover goods and property?

Are you going to war or in a war because you like to fight and keep something going? That's demonic, you know.

Are you interested in war to get someone else's stuff or goods? Is personal greed involved?

Whatever the reason, make sure it is sanctioned by God. Pray. Have you declared war on an evil entity? With permission? Under authority? Or is this unsanctioned?

My biggest question is that if Jesus told us to forgive 70 X 7 times even in the same day, when does forgiveness *stop* and **war** begin? Of all the things the Bible tells us to forgive if taken away from us, none of the above losses are listed as things we should forgive.

But I say unto you which hear, Love your enemies, do good to them which hate you, Bless them that curse you, and pray for them which despitefully use you.

And unto him that smiteth thee on the one cheek offer also the other; and him that taketh away thy cloak forbid not to take thy coat also.

Give to every man that asketh of thee; and of him that taketh away thy goods ask them not again.

And as ye would that men should do to you, do ye also to them likewise. For if ye love them which love you, what thank have ye? for sinners also love those that love them. Luke 6:27-32

At what point do you stop forgiving a person? Never? Then how is war ever declared on anyone? Any people? Any country?

Then how do wars even get started? How is war declared? Does the child of God never declare war, never make war, or do saints of God only forgive? What if war comes up to a saint's doorstep?

Do we Christians only forgive people who ask for forgiveness, or do we offer a blanket of forgiveness to all people, 24/7?

Those who presented to Jesus for healing and deliverance whether they realized it or not were asking for forgiveness of sins **and** the iniquity of those sins. Jesus forgave those who asked.

Jesus forgave the whole world their sins when He went to the Cross. Some had sought forgiveness, and some would be seeking forgiveness in the *future*. GOD KNEW. But most people of that day were NOT seeking forgiveness. Jesus forgave all, even those who didn't ask, too.

Unrepentant enemies do not ask forgiveness. Yet we are expressly told in the Old Testament not to make alliances with the enemies of God.

Do not make a covenant with them or with their gods. Exodus 23:32

Stay away from people who are not followers of the Lord! Can someone who is good get along with someone who is evil? Are light and darkness the same? (2 Corinthians 6:14 CEV)

Asking for and giving forgiveness is making a contract. It is making an alliance. What concord does dark have with light?

Jesus said, *Father, forgive them for they know not what they do.*

An unrepentant sinner, a confirmed witch or a warlock, for example, is NOT ignorant of what they are doing. They are practiced, taught, studied. First, they schemed up revenge or some other plot in their minds, and then gone out and gotten the weirdest items to create hexes, vexes and curses on their victims.

They **know** what they are doing, and they know the desired outcomes against their chosen victims. If you let them talk, they will brag about what they are going to do, and the horrible results that will be the outcome of their actions. They know. Their words and actions are a declaration of war against their intended victim.

If you're the victim and you figure out that war has been declared on you – that this is not just stuff that *happens*, or coincidence, you still should seek wise counsel before engaging in war. Many times, that wise counsel is the Lord. Pray. Listen. Then, act.

Every purpose is established by counsel: and with good advice make war. (Proverbs 20:18)

For by wise counsel thou shalt make thy war and in multitude of counsellors there is safety.
(Proverbs 24:6)

Don't go to war without first asking and hearing from God and any other wise counsel that God sends you to, or to you because when God sends you into battle the victory is assured. For there fell down many slain, because the war was of God. And they dwelt in their steads until the captivity. (1 Chronicles 5:22)

Is this war of God? Is God sending you out to war on behalf of the Kingdom? For yourself? Are you in intercession, assisting someone else? Men banded together is powerful, where two or three are gathered together, the Lord is in the midst if God has approved the action.

Ask God anything. Ask as David did regarding Ziklag, *Shall I pursue? And if I pursue, will I recover all?*

God empowers His sons, His warriors for battle because He trusts you with power. He trusts you with weapons. You've been trained and you've been made ready. God has never been defeated and never will be.

Thou art my battle axe and weapons of war for with thee I will break in pieces the nations and with thee I will destroy kingdoms; (Jeremiah 51:20).

The Battle

And of the Danites expert in war.

1Chronicles 12:35

To be excellent warriors, sons of God need to be well-versed with instruments of war. Do not go out to war unless you are expert with your weapons and instruments.

If you need strength, ask God. The Captain of the Hosts of the Armies of the LORD will fight with you; He will fight for you and give you victory in battle.

And I saw heaven opened and behold a white horse; and he that sat upon him was called Faithful and True, and in righteousness he doth judge and make war. (Revelation 19:11)

Wars begin with a battle. The declaration of war is made because a **judgement** is made or won. God has the power and authority to make **judgements of war.**

When forgiving is no longer a course of action, we present our case to God at the Throne of Grace. We present our case using Courtroom Prayers which is a style of prayer. This is what the devil is doing *against* us day and night, accusing mankind before God, hoping that God would declare war on His creation because the devil knows we wouldn't have a chance if that happened. But God is merciful, tenderhearted, longsuffering, forgiving, giving us Grace and Mercy.

For this reason, God does not declare war on humans, but we need to present our own courtroom cases to the Lord at the Throne of Grace if we want to receive a judgment from God against the enemies of God.

After that, we may legally, with Heavenly support wage war against the Evil that's in this Earth and in our own lives sometimes.

Throughout seasons of war, stay prayerful and continue to ask God for what you need and be sure to listen to hear God's voice.

If you need courage, ask God for it, as in Psalms 27:3.

Though an host should encamp against me, my heart shall not fear; though war should rise against me, in this will I be confident. (Psalm 27:3)

If you need help, ask for help. Know what verse or verses you are standing on in a *Season of War.*

God hath spoken once; twice have I heard this; that power belongeth unto God, (Psalm 62:11)

And he shall set engines of war against thy walls, and with his axes he shall break down thy towers.
Ezekiel 26:9

It's Quiet Now

Don't be lulled into a false rest: if you're *not* currently in a season of war. Every season should be a time of prayer, praise and worship to God. There is never nothing to do, spiritually. There is always something to do in the natural and also spiritually. Do not think because you don't see anything actively happening that nothing is happening. You can pray prayers of preparation so you are not caught flat-footed by some demonic scheme.

You could be praying prayers of a preventive nature to KEEP the enemy at bay. Prayers of protection are excellent for that. Jesus said, *"Occupy until I come."* That means stay busy and be busy doing the Lord's work until Jesus returns.

Woe unto those who are at ease in Zion.

In whatever season you find yourself, keep serving God. You could be going through a *season of war* where a bow of steel is broken in your arms. God is strengthening you.

He teacheth my hands to war so that a bow of steel is broken in mine arms, (2 Samuel 22:35).

Pray—

Lord, thank You for the privilege of coming before Your Throne of Grace to find help in this season, in time of need. Lord, I saw in Your Word that the enemy may come up against us like a flood. And in Your Word, You said You would raise up a standard against them.

- Father, whatever plans the enemy has against me, whatever he has released against my life, let the Earth open Her mouth and swallow the floodwaters, those proud waters that are trying to overtake me, in the Name of Jesus.

Amen—

Grace

God is raising up sons. Prophetically we are sons, so we are under Grace. The servant is under the Law, but the son is under Grace. Guests in your home have rules that your children don't have to abide by. Your children have Grace. Guests sit down and if offered a beverage, they wait until it is brought to them. If your child wants juice, they just go to the kitchen, open the fridge and get it.

While God's Grace is sufficient for us, in some seasons we may need *more* Grace. In seasons of warfare pray for Grace to go *through,* trusting in God. Have faith in God, knowing full well that you have the victory, in the Name of Jesus.

Pray—

- You are God, all by Yourself, and bigger than anything that I could ever confront or that could ever confront me, in the Name of Jesus. Lord, thank You for allowing me to go victoriously through this *season of war.*

- I bind the *spirits of weariness, fatigue, tiredness,* in the Name of Jesus.
- Lord, thank You for allowing me a season of rest after this *season of war.*

But they that wait upon the LORD shall renew their strength; they shall mount up with wings as eagles; they shall run, and not be weary; and they shall walk, and not faint. Isaiah 40:31

Amen—

So that whatever happens Lord, I am, as a son of God, I'm prepared. All Creation is moaning and groaning for the Sons of God to appear because the whole world, the whole Earth needs deliverance.

Pray—

I praise you Lord for You are worthy of praise, and there's nothing too difficult for You, Father.

I bind the *spirits of discouragement, fear,* and *doubt,* in the Name of Jesus.

Lord, place a strong *spirit of praise* and *prayer* on me, even in this season so I do not become dry and brittle without the Word and without prayer. Lord I will continue to praise Your Name because You are God all by Yourself.

You're worthy and You are mighty. You are my Savior; You are my Redeemer.

The Name of the Lord is a strong tower, the righteous rush in, and they are safe.

Amen—

Incoming!

During seasons of war, the Devil uses *anybody*. He will use **people** to speak words of discouragement to shut you down. Friends, families and people who are usually well-meaning may give you their stories of fear and doubt and may try to convince you to stop or give up.

They may want you to party (sin) with them to take your mind off of your problems. Without meaning to, they may end up pulling you away from God. Some people don't even know when they are being used by the devil.

Some know exactly what they are doing and intend to interrupt your God-connection to watch you fall. Pulling you away from God, can start with distracting you from your prayer time. These are the enemy's chief goals, as he plans your destruction.

Once you sin – once you become defiled or defile yourself, then the devil has *access* to you.

Once you sin and don't repent, the devil **really** has access to you.

Whatever you use to sin *with* is the usual access point. And it is often what will be under attack.

You might not sin, but the bloodline you were born into is corrupted/polluted – that may have been the access the devil had to you.

No Mercy

While you're going *through*, the devil doesn't stop. Mercy is not in the devil's vocabulary – so in this **Season of War** ask God for Mercy for yourself and your bloodline, as you call for judgment on the enemies of God. This is war; war has been declared on you.

Defend yourself. Be ready, make ready to defend yourself.

The devil will use anyone who's susceptible, even someone who is saved sanctified, and set aside. Anyone~~, your closest relative, your closest friend, co-worker. Anyone. Even your child. It could be someone who usually gives you Godly counsel, but now they've changed up on you.

This is why you must *discern* the *spirit* of who's speaking, not just the who of who's speaking. Not what they look like, and not what their voice sounds like, or even what they mean to you, but the *spirit* and the **intent** behind what they are saying to you. Be objective. Ask yourself, Is this something that God would say? Is this in the Word of God? Did Jesus ever say anything like this?

Be wise and discerning. It could be *not God* at all.

Peter said that he didn't want Jesus to have to go to the Cross and be crucified and Jesus said, ***Satan, get thee behind Me*** (Matthew 16:23). It was Peter talking, it was Peter standing there in the flesh, but Jesus *discerned* who was speaking, and called that devil out. It may be tough but while you are going *through* you still have to keep your wits about you to even be able to use your spiritual gifts, such as discernment.

Do not go into your flesh. That is what the devil wants. In your flesh your spiritual gifts do not work, either at all, or as they should. Most of the gifts work by love. In your **flesh** there is NO LOVE. In your flesh is only physical strength and works of the flesh.

Once you discern who is behind what is happening to you, and the devil is behind your problems, then you take it to God and ask for judgment against the enemy. At that point the war either starts or you're allowed to get in there and defend yourself, your family and your property. Don't stop praying when you're under attack. If you were in a dry season or have never started praying, now is the time to start.

If the devil is using people to attack you, *you* still must stay in the *Spirit.* Do not come down into the flesh, because you will start attacking **people**. That's a no-no.

Stay in the Spirit because **the flesh cannot fight spirit.** The devil is spirit. This is why we must build up *our* spirit man. Our defense is in the Spirit, not the flesh. Abide in prayer, praise, seeking God, studying the Word and practicing the disciplines of the faith.

Don't stop praying or seeking the face of God when you're under attack. Keep your prayer altar hot. Never let it cease or dry up or become desolate. **The Devil's target is your prayer life which is your communication with God. The enemy's target is your faith and your connection with God; if he can break**

that, you're a goner. You're supposed to be a son of God, not a goner.

Pray—

- I take authority over every *spirit of discouragement and fear. Lord, You've not given us the spirit of fear, but one of love, power and a sound mind.*
- By help of the Holy Spirit, I resist every negative thought the enemy sends.

I tie every one of my thoughts to the obedience of Christ. I cast down every negative thought that the enemy has been releasing into my life, against my destiny, life, purpose, ministry, career, family, business, in the Name of Jesus.

Lord, give me discernment of *spirits* to know when *people* are being used by the devil against me in this war.

Lord, give me accurate dream interpretation and send me to right sources to get true Biblical interpretation if I don't know. Holy Spirit, teach me. Allow me to see through masquerades in the dream, especially during this **season of war.**

- Every arrow that is targeted at my peace, return to sender, in the Mighty Name of Jesus Christ.

Father, I declare that my life, my body my house, work, everything under my stewardship is a NO-FLY zone for evil arrows, witches, warlocks and astral projectors, from this day forward, in the Name of Jesus. (repeat many times)

- Shield of faith, repel every fiery dart of the enemy. All evil darts, ricochet, boomerang, fly back to sender--, especially arrows of affliction, arrows of death, in Jesus' Name.

All plans of the enemy to use people that are closest to me to discourage me to help the enemy out in any way, I command those plans to be canceled and destroyed in Jesus' Name.

- I reject every negative *spirit* after my life, my situation, in the Name of Jesus.

Amen—

Seasons of Tests

In the *season of tests,* God is still with you. Promotion comes from the Lord; promotions come from passing tests. In testing seasons God knows what you're going through. Don't pull away from God. Do not become weary, we *will* become *sons* of God.

If a man lacks Wisdom, let him ask God who will give it liberally.

If we need Wisdom, we ask God. And, ask God for the battle plan to go into this **Season of War.** Also ask God to show you the plans of the enemy against you, in the Name of Jesus. You've asked for knowledge, nowt that you have the war plans, now ask for Wisdom to know how to USE those plans and/or how to defend yourself.

If you need comfort, the Holy Spirit is our Comforter.

Our light and momentary troubles are achieving for us an eternal glory that far outweighs them all. So we fix our eyes not on what is seen, but on what is unseen, since what is seen is temporary, but what is unseen is eternal.

(2 Corinthians 4:17-19)

You are probably in a ***season of warfare*** because you are doing something that the devil either doesn't like or is worried about. Gird up. Mount up. Get prayed up, bring your warfare up to the next level.

This war in the heavenlies, is over you, it's ABOUT you—and me. Yes, it really is about you. We have been given the authority to become a *son* of God. God is raising up sons and the devil doesn't like it at all. The war is about YOU and about your becoming a son of God.

Maintain your prayer life. Step it up, actually. Put on the whole armor of God. Stand firm. Stand therefore.

The devil doesn't want you to reach that destiny. The heavenly wars that spill over into the Earth realm that we feel so uncomfortably in our flesh…are about *us*. It's about us because God is raising up sons and demonic opposition can be fierce.

Our struggle is not against flesh and blood even though both unsuspecting and/or evil human agents are being used by the devil.

Trained to Lose

Prepare war, wake up the mighty men, let all
the men of war draw near; let them come up.
(Joel 2:9)

There was a man who didn't believe in
witchcraft, *while* he was under full attack of
witchcraft and in complete denial. All-out
war had been declared against him, by a
household witch, but he couldn't see it. So, he
spent his days, and money looking for natural
solutions to spiritual health issues. The witch,
or witches, if there was a coven, were having
a field day with him. He muddled along in
middle age, going into his senior years
wondering why his "body was falling apart."
But, naturally speaking, his body was not
falling apart, at least no doctors could find
much wrong with him.

No person had laid a hand on him, this
was all spiritual; this was witchcraft. It was a
household witch.

If he had known, he may not have fought back anyway.

Their parents taught him to **always** forgive; he would have forgiven her while she shot arrows of affliction and death at him. Obviously, she didn't believe the same parental lessons of forgiveness and kindness applied to her.

Worse, this man was **supporting** the *weapon* formed against him, he worked and paid the bills in that household while the witch lunched and planned evil against him--, and any female that he may have been interested in. The household witch cared for *money* more than her relative.

The man or woman who won't fight in a war is a **victim**. Easy prey. They are trained to lose. When witches want revenge or something you have and you don't fight, outside of the Mercy of God they will win, especially if you are forgiving them, asking Mercy for them and not for yourself. When what you've trusted in cannot sustain you in spiritual battle, defeat is imminent. You trusted Mom, Dad, your Sunday school teacher who all said to always forgive.

What does God say? Jesus said, **Father, forgive them for they know not what they do.** If everyone automatically forgave everyone else would there be a Court of Law? Would there be Courts in Heaven? There would never be wars. God is not behind every war, but many times in the Bible He sent people to war and said, *Completely destroy the enemy.*

The man under witchcraft was obeying his parents by making and keeping a covenant of forgiveness with the household witch/family member. If you're the only one in a covenant, it's not a covenant.

The witch had other plans.

Mighty Warrior

The LORD shall go forth as a mighty man, he shall stir up jealousy like a man of war: he shall cry, yea, roar; he shall prevail against his enemies. Isaiah 42:13

Mighty warrior! Mighty warrior. God is raising up sons and teaching our hands to war.

The glory of war is not the battle, nor is it the violence. The glory of war is the victory. The glory of victory is taking your enemy captive, expelling them, exiling them, or completely destroying them. That's the glory of the victory. And the glory of the victory is the spoils, such as the peace, where you dwell in safety because of the enemy's defeat. There is also glory in the value of spoils taken and recovered in victory.

Jesus defeated the devil and took captivity captive, making a spectacle of the devil. Then He gave gifts unto men. To the victor, the spoils.

The God of the Bible, the God and the Father of our Lord Jesus Christ is the Almighty God, and He is Jehovah Sabaoth. Jehovah Sabaoth was first mentioned in 1 Samuel 1:3 where Hannah cries out to God for a son. Hannah was being tormented by her husband Elkanah's *other* wife, Peninnah, who was tormenting her because Hannah had no son.

When we war as we're supposed to, spiritually we are made, sons of God, Mighty warriors. When we are sons of God, we also war spiritually because of having been raised up to be like Abba, Father.

Hannah had no son. And before His only begotten son, God also had no sons. Peninnah was tormenting and accusing Hannah just as the devil surely stands at the throne of God, day and night, accusing the brethren.

I imagine he might say, *That creation you made, look at what they're doing now. Adam, he's henpecked. Eve, well, that was no challenge. She was like a silly woman. No challenge at all.* Day and night. The Accuser of the Brethren standing, accusing God's creation, accusing mankind.

Don't you have kids that you want to be proud of? You don't want somebody making fun of your children, do you--, accusing them day and night? Neither does God.

So I believe that God heard Hannah's prayer for two very important reasons. As the devil was using Peninnah to curse Hannah in the natural and himself accusing her at the Throne of God, Hannah went to the temple and because she prayed, she did not let the devil's accusations go unanswered. That is critical because a lot of humans do not pray, they do not bow down to God in prayer, therefore the enemy's accusations go unanswered. Jesus is our Intercessor and Advocate and will speak on our behalf at the Throne of God, but if we don't participate in our own defense, how can we expect to <u>win</u> in seasons of tests or war?

Peninnah's torment of Hannah was a reflection of the warfare at the Throne of Grace which was *war* against Hannah. Even though the priests thought Hannah was a mad woman, she defended herself spiritually and won the victory. Samuel the Prophet was God's answer to Hannah. Quite a spoil, wouldn't you say?

Secondly, because God hears us, He hears our prayers, and God's heart was moved with compassion because God wanted *sons* that He could be well pleased about.

God doesn't ask us to do anything that He Himself would not do. He says, *Be fruitful and multiply*. And that's a third reason why I also believe God heard and honored Hannah's prayer. God wants sons, and He wanted many sons. He wanted to be fruitful Himself and multiply.

And it came to pass in those days, that Jesus came from Nazareth of Galilee, and was baptized by John in the Jordan. And straightway coming up out of the water, He saw the heavens opened, and the Spirit like a dove descending upon Him. And there came a voice from Heaven saying. Thou art my beloved son, in whom I am well pleased. Thou art my son. This day have I begotten thee, (Psalm 2:7).

We know this because God knew them in advance, and he decided in advance that we would be conformed to the image of His Son. (Rom 8:29 CEB)

That way, His Son would be the first of many brothers *and sisters*.

Prophetic Battles

In 1 Samuel 17:4 David comes out against Goliath in the Name of the Lord, Jehovah Sabaoth. Recall that story and know that what is happening in the natural is a reflection of what is happening in the Spirit. They say David was a young lad at that time, like Daniel. Why would a *whole* giant, an accomplished, well-seasoned warrior who had scared away many other warriors oppose David? **It's because of who David was to GOD.**

Think of the level of the opposition against you in your life--, so far. I know I've said, *What did I do to deserve this,* more than once in my life. Saints of God, sometimes your season of war is a **prophetic battle.**

- The *who* you are *to God* is **called** to that battle.
- The *who* you are being trained up to be is called to that battle.

- The *who* you will be because of this battle is who will be revealed at the end of that prophetic battle.

God is raising up sons, He is teaching our hands to war and fingers to fight. Don't reject your **seasons of war**, if God is allowing it, He has purpose in it.

In 2 Kings 6, Elijah is running from the King of Aram and the king sends an entire army against the Prophet and his armor bearer--, just two people. Jehovah Sabaoth showed up to defend them.

There were just two people, but the king sent an entire army against them. Ironic because as strong as Elijah was *in the Spirit*, no flesh army could conquer him. In the heavenlies, the devil and the evil king in the natural were afraid enough to send an entire army after two people. After seeing the great exploits Mt. Carmel.

Elijah, on the other hand, had just defeated 450 prophets of Baal, but then he ran scared of Jezebel to hide. Elijah went into his flesh. Elijah and his armor bearer were just two little people--, **in their flesh.** God too will send the Hosts of the Army of the Lord. He will send an entire Army. He will move Heaven and Earth for *one*. He does not wish that one would be lost, but He'll do it for you if you are His *son*.

Absolutely

Jehovah Sabaoth is a mighty warrior. He's Sovereign, He's supreme. He controls the *visible and invisible* angelic Hosts of the Armies of the Lord. He's the Sovereign God. He rules Heaven and Earth, and His power is absolute.

A warring king cannot stay home during the battle. He can't sit at home during the war. When a soldier is trained for battle and he doesn't go out and fight his enemies, he may fall into sin, as David did; that's when he saw Bathsheba.

A battle-ready soldier who doesn't fight as God directs will fall into sin of some kind. If he fights friends or family, that's sin. It is only not sin if that man has a judgment from God against known or proclaimed enemies, else he should be forgiving them.

A Christian, *warrior king* cannot just sit on a pew in the church, continuing to get the same instructions over and over again. He needs to do battle--, spiritual battle.

And in the natural a warring king can't sit home and TV binge, chill all day and all night. He must go to war.

The glory of war is the victory, and it is the spoils.

David's Men

These are three of David's mighty warriors: Josheb, Eleazar, and Shammah.

Josheb raised his spear against 800 men whom he killed in one encounter, (2 Samuel 23:8).

Eliazar stood his ground and struck down the Philistines till his hand grew tired and froze to the sword. The Lord brought a great victory that day. And the troops returned to Eleazer, but only to strip the dead, (2 Samuel 23:10)

And next to him was Shammah. And Shammah took his stand in the middle of the field. He defended it and struck the Philistines down. And the Lord brought about a great victory.

(2 Samuel 23:14)

Some of these were some of the exploits of the three mighty warriors of David.

David, Chief among them, was later promoted to king. Mighty warriors who win, rule, reign, and are promoted.

In the natural, men fight for *things* and *stuff.* In the Old Testament especially, they fought for land and territory. But they also fought also for their lives, for safety, and to protect their families. I call these external wars.

The War for Men's Souls

Jesus came from Heaven to Earth because of a war, because of the war for men's souls. What does it profit a man if he gains the whole world, if he has *things* and *stuff,* but loses his soul?

Jesus taught us to pray, *Let it be done on Earth, even as it's done in heaven.*

In the Book of Revelations, it tells us that a war was declared in Heaven, and we've discussed how Heaven and Earth goings-on often reflect one another. Jesus came from Heaven to Earth because of the war for men's souls, the war for man's very life. Every man.

Jesus came here to do battle for all of us-- , all mankind. Jesus, the Mightiest of Warriors binds up broken hearts, heals the sick, feeds the hungry, redeems lost mankind back to the Father and took captivity captive because He is a warrior.

Mankind, in Adam had sinned and wandered off from his purpose and his destiny, and he and all mankind had to be returned, and redeemed back to the Father.

Then, in the New Testament, the prodigal son wandered off and had to return back to his Father.

In between Adam and the prodigal son are the prophetic words of God given through Malachi.

But unto you that fear my name shall the son of righteousness arise with healing in his wings, and he shall grow up.

Thou shalt tread down the wicked. For they shall be ashes under the soles of your feet..
(Malachi 4:2-3a)

Jesus came to fulfill that Word. We're supposed to be like Jesus. In everything that you and I go through in this life, God is teaching us. He's teaching us to reign after we win the war. Historically, the king of any country, province, area, territory was a warrior. The Lord is a warrior, the Lord is His name.

We're supposed to be like God, like Jesus. We're supposed to be little *kings* in the Earth. Are we taking advantage of our preparation that the Lord is sending us through and in our walk?

We shall reign with Christ Jesus in the afterlife. But what about the life we're living now? We also know from the way that Jesus taught that *it is finished*, the war is won, and the victory secured.

The Memo

Here is a glimpse into how divine timing works. By the time Jesus got to Earth, in the flesh, the Lamb of God had already been slain.

The devil had already been defeated. The devil knows this, but he gaslights mankind into believing that he's not defeated. Unfortunately, some humans believe this. Some people just don't know. Some think the devil is a victim, and he was kicked out of the house unfairly.

Oh my God. Please read your Word.

The American Civil War was over, and the Emancipation Proclamation had been signed on January 1, 1863, but it took until Juneteenth 1865 for everyone to get the message. So, from 1863 till Juneteenth 1865, mankind was still *walking out* the Civil War because everyone didn't yet know that the war was actually over.

And still.

Did I mention that the American Civil War is over? OK.

Jesus, on Calvary was our *spiritual* **emancipation** from the devil and from the Curse of the Law. He liberated us from the Law of Sin and Death before the foundation of the world. People of God, it was the *emancipation* for our souls, our bodies, our very lives.

The Devil is already defeated, but we have to do our parts, *Mighty Warriors* of God. We have to walk this out.

God says, while you are yet praying, I will answer.

And it shall come to pass that before they call I will answer, and while they are yet speaking, I will hear. (Isaiah 65:24)

We have already been saved; we need to walk it out. If we don't want to get ahead of our destiny clock, then we are subject to Divine timing. Jesus has healed us already by stripes and by Calvary, (Isaiah 53:5). God has already answered, we just have to walk it out. Divine timing. Everything is already done. Everything is already won. It's just up to us to walk it out.

God is far ahead of us in His answer, and we have to *catch up.*

God delivered the Israelites out of Egypt--, out of Egyptian slavery with a mighty deliverance, but it took them 40 years to reach the Promised Land. It took a lifetime. It took half a lifetime. It took a long time to reach the Promised Land. And this land had already been given by God. God had already answered them; it already been secured for them; it was just a matter of Divine timing.

The Slow Way

Mankind, we've got choices. We can obey God and things can go reasonably evenly for us, reasonably fast, or we can invite sin in, and delay, risk or completely miss destiny. By disobedience and rebellion, we can slow things down and have opposition, oppression, battles, and wars, or we can obey God.

We have free will; we have choice. Yet in that choice, in God's Mercy He still teaches our hands to war. God gives us the choice to learn it His way or the slow way. What we need, what we ask for, He's already done it for us. He's already given it to us. He's already secured it for us. Then our way is really **slow**. So how smart are we to take the slow way?

God doesn't look on sin. So if we're choosing sin and taking the slow road, God's not in that. That's why sin slows things down so much. Because when God is not in a thing, you're either going nowhere or worse, you're going backward.

Deliverance

Humans, even Christians, need deliverance, like those in the wilderness who still needed to be *delivered* into the Promised Land. Those in the wilderness were in idolatry, rebellion, grumbling, and complaining--, you know, sinning--, because that's more fun than obeying God. *Really?*

Sometimes we think the little sins aren't sins, but they are. And they slow things down because the devil gets into all sin, even the little sins. Sin is sin.

So, whoever said that Christians don't need to be delivered needs to talk to Amazon, UPS, FedEx, and God first, because everything needs to be *delivered.* If that package can't walk itself through the wilderness into the Promised Land, then somebody will have to go get it.

If all of the 600,000 or more, maybe up to three or four million Israelites, depends on how you count them, that came out of Egypt couldn't seem to get themselves out of a wilderness, into the Promised Land, then they needed a deliverer.

Why do you think God sent us a deliverer? A war is a wilderness that we need deliverance from. Ideally, deliverance should come at conversion to Christ. That would be the most convenient way, wouldn't it? But it doesn't always happen that way. Because things hide. People hide. People hide their sins. New sins come upon people, every day, because of unforgiveness, bitterness, anger, hurt—just living life. Diseases hide in the human body. Anything can hide, or try to hide.

Don't you look for a tick on your dog because ticks hide. They don't just drop off your dog automatically because it is *your* dog.

We sometimes need help getting from Point A to Point B. We need help transitioning to the *next level*. We need help, and God sends us help, deliverance.

Don't you go to the doctor when you have symptoms to discover the disease and be rid of it? Or do you just wait for the symptoms to stop and never take an Advil or Tylenol? Pain meds are forms of help until you can get the full deliverance--, a diagnosis, a procedure, and a stronger prescription. So don't say you don't believe in deliverance.

If we don't have any more discipline than to take the slow route when God has clearly outlined the most expedient route to our successes and destiny, then we need a deliverer. If we constantly slow things down by sinning, Lord, help us. Send a Deliverer.

Jesus Christ is our mighty deliverer who has ultimately delivered us out of bondage and delivered us from sin and death. It is *done*, but we have to walk it out.

Spirits hide, demons hide in a person, and it's not until the *symptoms* are seen or felt that anyone would even think that they need deliverance. So, if we sin and don't confess and repent of it, instead of trying to hide it, we delay or completely risk our destiny.

Discerning spiritual symptoms from natural symptoms takes God. It takes prayer. It takes an ear to hear what the Lord is saying.

Christian rules of conduct are in the Bible. How a Christian should act--, they're all in there. As long as a Christian can *act* like a Christian most people will never think they need help. It is only by Holy Spirit discernment will anyone know. Some unsaved people convincingly *act* like Christians in public, especially at church.

Pharisees *acted*. But we're supposed to be for real, right? Not pretending, not being Christian-like, but being **real** Christians.

Still, there's anger and bitterness, unforgiveness, rage, insecurity, thoughts of suicide, thoughts of homicide, *lying spirit,* murder, adultery, ideology, dissension, division--, all works of the flesh. As long as a person can consistently **act,** no one will ever notice that they need deliverance.

Sometimes these *spirits* take over and deliverance is needed. A person may notice on their own that they need deliverance. That can be tough, because all the ways of a man are clean and pure in his own eyes, (Proverbs 16:2).

That is one of the reasons why we have the Holy Spirit. The Holy Spirit convicts. One must be convicted of sin to recognize that they have a problem and change their ways and get prayer, or get into prayer. Prayer is **deliverance.** You're not gonna tell me you don't pray?

There are all kinds of prayer; every prayer is a cry for deliverance from something--, sickness, disease, poverty, worry. Prayer is deliverance, no matter if it's yelled from the rooftops or whispered softly. **Prayer is deliverance.**

In Seasons of War, the *acting* Christian is not participating in any warfare because they can't. The war is <u>*internal*</u> for the *actor.* When he sincerely confesses and repents, then he can start heading toward his destiny again. Until then, he is either standing still or going backward as the **war** overtakes him.

Jehovah Sabaoth

When God answers as Jehovah Sabaoth or Jehovah Shammah, whichever attribute He shows up in, **it's all deliverance.** God wants to reveal Himself to us. Every revelation of His attributes is all deliverance for us.

In converting from sinner to Christian, the sinner probably gives up and renounces every *symptom* that they **know** of. Depending on the person, they may give up every symptom that they *think others know of.* It depends on how truthful any sinner is at the time.

But the stuff that people think is working for them, the sins that they are enjoying, he may not easily give up or EVER be willing to give up. Anything that's feeding a man's flesh is really hard for that man to let go of. The sinner probably *gives up* every sin that is called out by the pastor or the Evangelist or whoever is administering salvation by Jesus Christ, through faith, by Grace. It could be an honest mistake; the sinner may not know enough at the time to know that they need to give up a whole lot of worldly stuff that is *not* called out at that particular moment.

When you think of the Cross and Jesus on that Cross, you realize that forgiveness is messy. There was a lot of blood associated with the crucifixion of Jesus. All that blood was for the forgiveness of our sins so that we can be saved, redeemed and put back in right relationship with the Father.

So a Sinner is converted to Christ in church. It's very neat and pretty and proper; it takes a few minutes, right? Forgiveness is immediate by Jesus Christ, but it is messy.

So we are to believe that a professional, *bona fide* sinner can invite Jesus into their heart, to be the Lord of their life, and their body becomes the temple of the Holy Spirit immediately, but no cleanup has to be done--, no remodeling, no redecorating?

You couldn't even buy a house and not want to change *something* about it--, the paint the décor-- *something.* We can't be arrogant and think that we're so perfect that Jesus will want to come in and not expect any kind of *change* in us.

The floors are all swept clean. By whom? Jesus. Well, Jesus is not the janitor; we clean up our own houses by fasting, by prayer, by resisting the devil, by going through deliverance.

You don't just clean your house one time when you move in and never again. We are the temple of the Holy Spirit, but some people have trouble receiving the Holy Spirit because they need deliverance first. Thank You, Lord for salvation *and* for deliverance.

God brought millions out of Egypt, yet they took the slow route and died not having seen the Promise. Don't miss the promise because of needing deliverance. It is the children's bread.

To become a son of God and also become a Mighty Warrior we have to submit to the Holy Spirit and also to deliverance at times.

Watchmen

God will send mighty warriors to deliver His people. One such mighty warrior is the Watchman on the wall, (Isaiah 62:6).

God has set Watchmen around the clock. God told Ezekiel, *I've made you a Watchman on the wall.* And he says,

> Whenever you hear a word from my mouth, you shall give them warning from me. If I say to the wicked, you shall surely die, and you give him no warning. Nor speak to warn the wicked from his wicked way, in order to save his life. That wicked person shall die for his iniquity. But his blood I will require of your hand. But if you warn the wicked, and he does not turn from his wickedness, or from his wicked way, he shall die for his iniquity, but you will have delivered his soul. (Ezekiel 3:17-19).

Sometimes the knowledge that deliverance is needed is spoken through a prophet of God, a watchman, an intercessor, these are others of God's Mighty Warriors.

But if the watchman sees the sword coming and does not blow the trumpet, so that the people are not warned, and the sword comes and takes any one of them, that person is taken away in his iniquity. But the blood I will require at the watchman's hand.
(Ezekiel 33:6)

This book is part of the warning. God has set Watchmen on the walls. He set watches in the night. And God knows who He has called to watch, to pray, and to *say*. The Watchman's watch IS warfare, it is a **Season of War** for that Watchman. Further, the Watchman warns and assists those for whom he is watching in *their* seasons, especially if the one being prayed for is in a **season of war**.

Their job is to speak it, and your job is to listen and obey the Word of the Lord. Every night the witching hour starts at midnight. But isn't it midnight somewhere, every day, all day, all night?

There are evil Council meetings between 12:00 am and 5:00 am. During those intervals, God has Watchmen that He wakes up, calling them to their posts to pray for you, the family, the community, the world, even the whole Earth. The Watchmen command the morning, command the day and they command the night. That doesn't mean that you shouldn't, also.

Be sober, watch and pray, put voice to the Words of God as you pray. If you are awake you are supposed to be praying. If you wake up at midnight, pray. If you wake up at 3:00 am, pray, 4:00 am--, any time that you consider an odd time, or unplanned time to be awake, it could be that the Holy Spirit has awakened you to pray.

I've got another whole deal going with God and I've prayed and asked the Lord to wake me up if anyone is enchanting against me. So if you're up at 3:00 am praying, I'm also up praying at that same time with you.

If you have an alarming dream and you wake up, that's why you had the alarming dream, so it would wake you up, so you would pray. Ezekiel was a permanent Watchman; you could be one called by God to be a Watchman. Or, you could go through a *season* where you wake up at 3:00 am every morning. You're a watchman whenever you are praying for others, no matter if it is temporary, for a season, or permanent.

Sometimes a person can walk in the *office* of prophet for a *season*, as did Saul when he was in the company of other prophets. Sometimes a person is called permanently to a particular *office* in the Lord.

In these **Seasons of War,** God is teaching our hands to war. He's teaching us to reign. Just as David, the chief warrior of his time was promoted to king. So shall we be raised up as sons and promoted to *little k kings* in the Earth.

When you're teaching your children, you give them chores that they can excel at. God is like that; He gives us things that we can do that we can win at as He raises us up as His *sons*.

You can pray.

You can wake up and pray.

You can stay up and pray.

Just pray.

The Mightiest Warrior

The mightiest warrior in the history of the world, the universe, eternity and infinity never lifted a man-made sword: Jesus Christ. Yet, He won it all.

For our God is a consuming fire, (Hebrews 12:29).

Chief of the Military arm of the Heavenly Hosts, Jesus *is* the Word; He is the sharp two-edged sword of God. When the Word comes out of His mouth against His enemies the King of Glory, Jehovah Sabaoth must come in, binding strongmen, crushing evil gates, and smashing demonic ancient doors. These battles cannot be fought in our human strength and energy, most definitely, never in our flesh.

We need You every hour, Lord, Mighty Warrior. The Lord is His Name. Jesus, the Mightiest Warrior, the Captain of the Host of the Armies of the Lord's Angelic Forces of Heaven and on Earth.

As a warrior, *you* have donned the entire spiritual armor of God, having your loins gird about with Truth, having on the breastplate of righteousness, your feet shod with the preparation of the Gospel of Peace, and the helmet of salvation. You take up the shield of faith, to quench the fiery darts of the wicked one. The Sword of the Spirit, which is the Word of God, praying always with all prayer in the Spirit. And watching there unto with all perseverance and supplication for all the Saints.

God's prophets and intercessors: thank you for your service, you are all **Mighty Warriors** who take on extra shifts and extra *Seasons of War.* God's Watchmen. Thank you for your service. To those who take the watches of the night 12 am to 3:00 am, and then 3:00 am to 6:00 am when evil flies against the people of God, when evil is unleashed and tries to upright itself to walk the Earth in the dark, while men sleep.

God sets watches and Watchmen against the foolish or desperate who call up Evil, thinking they can garner its power, or control it. They've got pestilence walking in darkness, destruction, terror, and arrows flying at noonday, as well as traps and snares to hurt, capture, or kill humans.

And it never stops. Until you stop it. Until you open your mouth and stop it, **Mighty Warrior.**

Those who watch and pray, we bless You. You are Mighty Warriors. You watch for yourselves, your own houses, for the community, for this nation, for this Earth. God's intercessors and prophets: Thank you.

Thank You, Lord Jesus.

The mighty warrior, Josheb raised his spear against 800 men, and those 800 men were killed in one encounter.

But Jesus the Christ raised His *voice* against 6000, whom He killed in one encounter. Those 6000, a *legion* in the Gadarenes were cast into the pigs, who then ran and jumped into the sea, because that's probably where they had come from-- e*vil marine spirits, evil marine demons.*

You, as a son of God have authority to cast out devils, heal the sick and set captives free.

Eleazer grew tired, and his hand froze to the sword, but he kept fighting.

Jesus, the Mightiest Warrior, appearing to be frozen to the Cross actually struck down all the work of the devil at Calvary. Then Jesus went to Hell and back, taking captivity captive, and He gave gifts unto men. He's the victor, therefore He received the spoils.

As the tongue is the pen of a ready writer, the Sword of God is the Word of God. Like Jesus we should give *voice* to the Word of God. Jesus consistently spoke the Word: *It is written. It is written. It is written.* Sharper than a two-edged sword. Jesus *is* the Word and He is the Sword of the Lord.

You too are a Mighty Warrior who has the Word of God in your mouth in season and out of season. You need to be ever ready to do battle *in prayer*, in decrees and declarations since you are a little *king* in the Earth, you are a *son* of God.

Speak. Using the Sword of the Spirit, the Word of God, speak; and then do all to stand, therefore.

Shammah took his stand in the middle of the field and defended it. He struck the Philistines down, and the Lord brought about a great victory.

The Mightiest Warrior, Jesus Christ, forever stands. He is our Intercessor, and He is a warrior; the Lord is His name.

<u>You</u> as a mighty warrior in the Earth, take your stand and stand, therefore.

Jehovah Shammah, the Lord is there. God is revealing Himself in another of His attributes.

When we war, we are made *sons* of God, and when we are sons of God, in the appropriate *season,* we war in the Spirit.

Hannah

Reviewing--, Hannah had no son. She was being mocked by Elkanah's first wife, Peninnah. God had no son, but like the devil that was in Peninnah, God was being berated by Satan. Not so much that He didn't have a son, but the devil was accusing mankind day and night before the Throne of God.

If the devil is justly accusing mankind, then the solution is that God needed a son or multiple sons that He could be proud of, pleased about, or at least not ashamed of. God's solution and Hannah's solution was the same.

God's not petty, but God wanted sons as well. The whole Earth is groaning and waiting for the *sons* of God to appear.

For the earnest expectation of the creature waiteth for the manifestation of the Sons of God.
(Romans 8:19)

Creation is still waiting. It yearns and burns. It scorches. It floods. It storms and quakes and tornadoes and hurricanes and monsoons. Creation cycles through the seasons. It hopes in the spring. Leaves fall like tears in autumn, waiting, yearning, praying for the Sons of God to appear.

Mighty Warriors of God. This day, the Lord says, I have begotten you. Mighty Warriors were such as Josheb, Eleazar, Shammah, David, Jesus of Nazareth. Jesus the Christ, firstborn of many brethren.

If you are in Christ, and He is in you. If you've been adopted, grafted in, and accepted in the Beloved, and you can discern the times and do spiritual battle in *Seasons of War*, add your name to that prestigious list.

But unto you that fear my name shall the sun of
righteousness arise with healing in his wings, and
you shall go for it, and grow up as calves of the stall.
And he shall tread down the wicked. For they shall
be ashes under the soles of your feet. In the day that
I shall do this, save the Lord of hosts. (Malachi 4:2)

Pray—

- Father God, as You have redeemed us from the Curse of the Law, by Jesus Christ and returned our hearts again to You, we pray that we are well pleasing to You.

- As You arise and fight on our behalf, on my behalf, Son of Righteousness, arise against Your enemies, against my enemies, against *our* enemies, the enemies of the Earth; I fight alongside You in the Spirit, in Christ Jesus.

You are the Lord of Lords. You are the Lord of the Heavenly and the Earthly Hosts; You are Jehovah Sabaoth.

We all are sons, and we all are daughters; there is no gender in You. Thank You, Lord. You call us mighty, I pray for and receive the *Spirit of Might* to be strong and very courageous so that I will be able to destroy the works of the devil, Quench the fiery darts, and evil arrows of the enemy.

You are the King of Glory, the Lord Strong and Mighty in battle. Mighty Warrior, Mightiest Warrior, the Lord is His name. Jehovah Sabaoth, Jehovah Shammah. Sons of God we are.

The Only Begotten Son of God, who is the firstborn of many brethren, many brothers, many sisters. Thank You, Lord, for counting us in that number.

We watch, we pray, we stand. We fight with the Word, the Sword of the Lord in our mouths, ready in season and out. With the sword like David's mighty warriors, Eleazer, whose hand froze to the sword, we will not let go of the Word, we will not let go of it.

Jehovah Shammah, *the Lord is there*. You are there with us, for us, by us, in us, and we are in You. In Christ Jesus we stand, we stand in the whole armor of God, and we stand therefore against spiritual wickedness in high places.

We smite the enemies of God, the enemies of our souls, the enemies of our health, strength, finances, peace, marriage, families, career, professions, safety, and livelihood.

Sun of Righteousness, arise with healing in Your wings. Against the wickedness in this Earth, we fight. Against household wickedness. Against wickedness seen and unseen. Against evil witchcraft and evil *spirits*. We will not be defeated.

Like David, against every Goliath, we come in the Name of the Lord of Hosts, we come in His Might. He is with us in every battle, every war. We tread down the wicked; they will be ashes under the soles of our feet, in the Name of Jesus.

We win. We win. This is the memo. We do not fret because of evil doers. We stand in array with the Captain of the Host of the Army of the Lord, and we do battle. In *Seasons of War*, we war as Mighty Warriors.

We are also Sons of God, and we do our purpose and our Calling, walking in our authority. We take up that sharp two-edged sword of the Lord which is the Word of God. We smite the enemies of our souls, the enemies of our spirits, the enemies of God, the enemies of our lives, destiny, and purpose.

We speak as with the voice of God, full of glory and strength. The voice of the Lord is upon the waters. The voice of the Lord Thunders. The voice of the Lord is powerful and full of Majesty. The voice of the Lord divides even flames of fire and shakes the wilderness.

God shakes the wickedness out of the Earth.

The Lord sits upon the flood, yay, the Lord sits King forever, and He is full of glory. All of our enemies are scattered, and we are never defeated. This enemy will never reassemble against us again. We shall see them no more. Mighty Warrior, warriors of God, never defeated, never defeated.

Who is the King of glory? It's the Lord. He's strong and mighty in battle, Jehovah, Sabaoth. We declare victory and peace to our lives, our homes, to all creation. Lord, thank You for giving us strength, and blessing us with peace on Earth. In the Name of Jesus, we pray.

Amen—

God says, While you are yet praying I will answer, (Isaiah 65:24).

But unto you that fear my name shall the Sun of righteousness arise with healing in his wings; and ye shall go forth, and grow up as calves of the stall.

And ye shall tread down the wicked; for they shall be ashes under the soles of your feet in the day that I shall do this, saith the LORD of hosts.

Malachi 4:2-3

Scatter Them

A war broke out in Heaven.

When we get the **revelation** of the *season* that we are in, realizing that we are in war, as in Heaven, we too will fight.

Forgiving 70 X 7, yes as the as the Lord instructs you, but when an enemy is also an enemy of God--, some *are not even human*. Some may try to deceive you over and again saying they are for peace when they love war. Some are strangers. Some are of the household of God. Some are of your mother's or your father's house. Some are of your own household.

They say peace, peace, but they are for war, (Psalm 120:7). There are some who imagine mischief and are continually gathered together for war; they could be in your workplace or rivals at your school or university (Psalm 140:2). We hope for and believe the best, but when we finally get the revelation that a person, or group of people not only do not mean us any good, but they also mean us harm, then we know we are in a battle. Prolonged battle is a **season of war.**

We visit *The Color Purple* to borrow Oprah Winfrey's character's famous line, *"You told Harpo to beat me?"* At that moment, Oprah's character realized **why** she had been in a war in her marriage. She thought Harpo was her enemy, and he was. Harpo *alone* was not the enemy. Spiritually that's like gang stalkers—gathered together. She needed a revelation to know how to defend herself, do battle, or flee to safety.

I am for peace but when I speak, they are for war. (Psalm 120:7)

We don't have to always know *who,* in the natural is coming against us. Sometimes we may not, since we do not war against flesh and blood. We just pray the *Whosoever* Prayer Battle, by Pastor Nnenna Akerele https://a.co/d/9OPK4mT

The Lord is a warrior, the Lord is His name. If your father is a warrior, a mighty man in battle, a conqueror, what do you think He will teach a *son*? Yes, how to be the same, how to be just like Him, to be conformed to His image.

He teacheth my hands to war so that a bow of steel is broken by mine arms. (Psalm 18:34)

The Lord will scatter your persistent, unrepentant enemies, those who insist on warring against you (Psalm 68:30). He is a warrior, but Jesus is also our Peace. Sometimes true Peace requires war, first. Yet He is Peace.

God teaches us seasons and times and how to conduct ourselves in every season.

As long as the Lord is in it, as long as you are in the Lord, the next season after war will always be victory.

If God is not in it, or you're in your flesh, as in an unsanctioned war, the next season may be captivity--, or worse. And there is no glory in that.

Glory is the Spoils

The glory of war is the spoils. The glory is to completely defeat your enemy, to tread upon the wicked as ashes under your feet.

The glory is the spoils. To recapture what is yours and/or to capture what is the enemy's are both spoils. To be repaid sevenfold times what was stolen from you is spoils. In this way the wicked will learn by having what they intended for you to happen to them. Or, even worse.

For the men of war had taken spoil, every man for himself, (Numbers 31:53)

The glory is the pleasure of living abundantly, and in safety and peace.   Surely the LORD gives us victory in every battle, and sanctioned war. He is never defeated and in Him, neither are we. The LORD is faithful to deliver.

In famine he shall redeem thee from death, and in war from the power of the sword. Job 5:20

There is at least one season in every man's life where he lives in peace and at rest, we should desire that it be perpetual. The season of rest is in the Lord and a gift from God. A man who no longer has to study war is a man blessed of God. Until then, we war.

Even a warrior must rest sometimes.

Let the praise of God be upon your lips, show Him worship. Praise and worship are prophetic, it indicates that you trust God to deliver you into a *promised* land, and that you prefer peace, you prefer rest instead of war.

Still there are seasons where you *must* war in order to win Peace. Enemies of God can be persistent, insistent, and relentless until they understand the POWER OF CHRIST. When they learn that **YOU** understand the power of Christ, know how to use it, and are willing to use it, they will flee from you. By enemies of God, we refer to actual humans who may also be influenced by wicked *spirits* that make war against the current and future *sons* of God.

The LORD will give you peace and allow you to beat your weapons of war into farm tools and live in safety.

… and they shall beat their swords into plowshares and their spears into pruninghooks, nation shall not lift up sword against nation, neither shall they learn war any more. (Isaiah 2:4b, Micah 4:3b.)

Season of Glory

Ask God to bring you through this **Season of War,** because there are other seasons in God, there are better seasons. There is a season of glory and there is a season of rest.

The Season of Glory is not a mirage. There is glory that is due God.

Pray—

- Lord, move me into the Season where You are magnified, and glorified. *Amen.*

There is a glory that is due man. We do not touch God's Glory.

The Glory of war is God receiving His glory. Everything God touches is glorious and victorious. To God be the Glory for all the things He has done for us.

Don't Stop

Pray—

Lord, I pray for Mercy for myself, and I pray for judgment against the powers behind my enemies. I pray against all attacks against my life, against my mind, my abundance, my health, purpose, ministry, strength, family, marriage, success, and peace.

Heavenly Father, every arrow of distraction that the enemy has introduced into my life, I return it to where it came from, in the Name of Jesus. I cover myself with the Blood of Jesus, and I cry MERCY!

I break and destroy every evil altar that the enemy is using to project negative *spirits* or curses against my life, in the Name of Jesus.

Thank You, Father, for the strength and stamina to endure, to be victorious in this war. Thank You for hearing and answering my prayers. All the glory, honor and praise belongs to You. *Amen.*

Never stop praying.

Praying *is* your WARFARE.

Whatever you were doing that the devil hates that caused him to put you in his sights, keep doing it. Maybe step it up during the attack. Conversely, whatever you were doing that kept God's hands of protection off you which allowed the attack, stop doing that.

Pray—

Father, strengthen me, so I do not fall in the day of adversity, in the Name of Jesus.

Lord, give more Grace, and the *spirit of prayer*, in Jesus' Name.

Lord, every *spirit* that is not like You and not from You, that is sent to stop my prayer life, whether it be sleep, slumber, or discouragement, I bind those *spirits,* in the Name of Jesus.

Holy Father, every arrow of sudden destruction, against my life--, every arrow of infirmity or affliction, return to sender.

By the power and the authority in the Name of Jesus, return every evil arrow to sender. Lord, release more Grace, the Spirit of Grace upon me, in every season.

Father, every *spirit of discouragement* that the enemy has sent to stop my prayer life I bind it, in the Name of Jesus.

Consuming Fire

Lord, destroy every horn that has made war against me, in the Name of Jesus.

Father, every arrow that the enemy has sent against my life to release infirmity, affliction, disease, or even death--, I reject every one of those arrows now, in the Name of Jesus. Return to sender.

No arrows of darkness can prosper against my life.

I declare that the shield the Lord has placed in my hands, will quench every fiery dart and arrow that the devil has, in Jesus' Name.

My God is a consuming fire. I unleash the fire of God upon every activity of the adversary against my life now, in the Name of Jesus.

Every evil power, principality and/or authority, that stands in the way of my victory in this season-- Fire of God--I call down the FIRE of God on you. Fire! Fire! Fire!

Lord, let Your Fire be released against them. Double Fire. Fire from Heaven, be released against them now, in Jesus' Name.

Today, blessings of health and divine healing are mine; I am made whole today by faith, in the Name of Jesus. This season of warfare against my health and destiny are OVER. By His stripes I am healed, Amen!

I declare today that financial blessings are coming to me in good measure, shaken together and running over. Today the season of financial warfare is over against my life and destiny, in Jesus' Name, Amen.

Thank You, Lord, for promotion and elevation in business. My career will enter into its next elevation. Thank You, Lord for an increase in prosperity and wealth, in Christ Jesus. Lord, I worship You and **not** mammon. I need Your help, Lord so that my daily focus is on YOU and not money, either the lack of it, the need for it, or the desire for it, or reveling in it, in the Name of Jesus.

Lord, by Jehovah Jireh, let all my needs be met according to YOUR riches in Glory. Jesus came that I may have life and have it more abundantly. Thank You, Father for the soul prosperity to handle abundance and not lust for it, or worship it, in the Name of Jesus.

Thank You Lord, that my marriage and relationships will enter into a new level, in the Name of Jesus.

Lord, thank You for every increase in education, career, jobs, marriage, family and children, in the Name of Jesus.

Lord, break me out of every limitation and constriction that is not of You. Thank You, Lord that I receive Godly things in Godly timing according to my clock of destiny and purpose, in the Name of Jesus.

Lord I pray MERCY for myself and ask for judgment against every priest or priestess at every evil altar and, all altars responsible for the *Season of Warfare* against my life. I pray that Your judgment come upon them in strange and mighty ways, in the Name of Jesus.

The enemy of this season, the enemies of my life must be defeated, in the Name of Jesus.

I have grown weary of this season, Lord; but I will not faint. You have strengthened me, You have encouraged me, You have comforted me, You have taught me, and with Your Mighty Right Hand You have made me to leap over walls, and through troops, taught my hands to war, my fingers to fight and caused me to do exploits.

Thank You for victory, complete and total victory in this season, in Jesus' Name. Amen.

I am a son of GOD – Lord, thank You for the Spirit of Might and for Grace in this season, teaching my hands to WAR, but also for raising me up, making me one of Yours and keeping me as the apple of Your eye.

There's no one like You, Lord in all the Earth. Nothing can compare. No one can compare to Your glory. ABBA, Father!

You are Holy, You're Righteous, You're God all by Yourself. I worship You, because You are God. I worship You in the Beauty of Your Holiness.

There is no arrow of darkness, sorrow, or affliction stronger than You, Lord.

There is no arrow that can penetrate the Shield of Faith that You've given me, and placed in my hand.

All the enemies are under Your feet; we tread on them like ashes and useless sand.

Thank You, Lord that I have tread upon the wicked. You give me power and authority to tread on the lion, the adder, the young lion, and the dragon. I trample them under my feet. You have made them like ashes under of my feet.

You, Lord are the Head of all and all. Higher than all principalities, all powers, all authorities in Heaven and Earth. Every knee must bow at the mention of that Name: Jesus. All power belongs to You.

Lion of the Tribe of Judah, You are the Beginning and End, the First and the Last, the Alpha and the Omega. You are All-Knowing, All Wise, Omnipotent, Omniscient God. You have all Wisdom; You know the End from the Beginning.

Thank You LORD, for making me a *son* of God, for defeating my enemies--, allowing me to defeat my enemies, for winning my battles and defeating the enemy for me, allowing me *victory, in* the Name of Jesus. Thank You for raising me up as a *son* of the Almighty God.

I bind the *spirit of retaliation* and close every access point by the Blood of Jesus. I seal these prayers and declarations in every realm, age, timeline, and dimension, past, present, and future--, to infinity in the Name of Jesus. *Amen.*

So Joshua took the whole land, according to all the LORD said unto Moses; and Joshua gave it for an inheritance unto Israel according to their divisions by their tribes.

And the land rested from war. (Joshua 11:23)
THE END

Christian books by this author

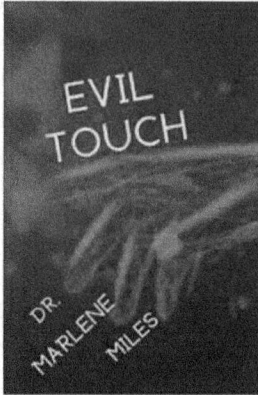

Find many more titles by this author, available on amazon, Kindle, and other platforms.